20 QUESTIONS
answered about
BEING A STAND-UP COMIC

10 answers you SHOULD know and 10 answers you MUST know

Veteran Comedy Stage Producer
R. Scott Edwards
tells all

Illustrated by Victoria Trum

20 Questions answered about Being A Stand-up Comic

© 2021, R. Scott Edwards

Edwards Publications

Self publishing

scottscomedystuff@gmail.com

ISBN: 978-1-09839-820-0

ISBN eBook: 978-1-09839-821-7

Dedicated to all the tremendous
Standup Comics I have had the
Pleasure to work with over the Years...
They are true Artist and Friends.
Oh,
and my Bride Jill...it was all her idea!

Edited
by
Mack Dryden
(a True Southern Gentleman)

Be Sure to check out

Online Comedy Course
Video Archive Memberships
&
My Podcast
Standup Comedy
"Your Host & MC"

www.scottscomedystuff.com

Preface

This book is from a **Comedy Producer's** point of view—I can't tell you how to be funny. But if you are, this book can transform you from an amateur to a paid professional.

I had the opportunity to work with true professionals like Jerry Seinfeld, Bob Saget, and Jay Leno, along with many more very funny people you may not have heard about: Steve Bruner, Bob Worley, Marc Yaffee, Milt Abel, Larry Wilson, Bruce Smirnoff, Tim Bedore, and many, many more!

You should be asking relevant questions to help YOU become a successful professional. Here are a LOT of the answers!

Sample from Chapter 18:

"I guarantee you, that if you work this through as this book explains, and do the writing, put in the stage time, and sell/sell/sell yourself; you WILL jump past others and succeed!"

TABLE OF CONTENTS

"BONUS" Chapter: How Do I Deal With Stage Fright?

Part One

10 Answers You Should Know

Chapter 1

Do I Need To Prepare?

All entrepreneurs, athletes, entertainers, actors, politicians, FBI agents, and professionals in every other field know the key to success is to follow the Boy Scout motto: *Be Prepared!* (even if you're not exactly a Boy Scout).

Proper preparation covers appearance, material, stage time filled, attitude on and off the stage, treatment of the staff, etc. You want to think through it *all* before you take the comedy stage.

Make sure you have written and practiced some material in front of a mirror, for family or friends, wherever makes sense. Never try going up cold—this isn't Karaoke! If this is something you *really want* to do, take it seriously. Go to a few shows first. Find out when Open Mic night is and what the crowd is like, how much time is allowed, and talk to staff and producer (if you can) and learn everything you can. Do the research!

You want to *Be Prepared* for the first one and *every* stage you hit (they're all a little different). Why? Because you only get ONE shot at making a First Impression—if you're unprepared and come off as a rank amateur, you'll set a precedent that the staff and producer will remember. They won't expect you to be a pro at an Open Mic, but they *will* expect you demonstrate that you prepared and took it seriously and not a *goof.*

Your attitude before and on the stage carries a lot of weight. If you are happy, helpful, energized, and excited, then the staff, audience, and other comics will see and feed off that. Everyone will *want* you to succeed. And even if you don't, they will support you and continue to be on your team and root for you.

Be Confident & Prepared!

Chapter 2:

Does It Matter What I Look Like On Stage?

This may sound simple, but you *must* put some thought into it. Why? Because who you *appear* to be when you take the stage carries weight with the producer, the staff, and the audience. Sorry, but people DO judge a book by its cover. How you dress is as important as your attitude. It's an extension of who you want to be on stage—the real YOU.

Some famous and very wealthy comics (Jerry and Jay) wear suits on stage, some like Emo Phillips or Goldthwaite have a specific look, and others establish themselves as the guy next door (Ray Romano & Dana Carvey). They all worked for me, and they all made sure that what they wore on stage was exactly the persona they wanted to present to the audience.

Sure, you have to dress appropriately for the venue and event. A suit is good for TV or a professional corporate show but will look stiff at an Open Mic. Nice clean jeans and button-down shirt still projects a comfortable yet professional look. Carlin *earned* that black t-shirt and jeans look, and you might pull it off if you're slim and fit and there are no visible ketchup stains.

I started out as an Emcee in a suit because I wanted the respect of the audience. Then later, when I had earned their respect and was more comfortable onstage, I was able to slowly adjust my look to jeans and Hawaiian shirts because I put in the time and earned it with my professionalism onstage.

I am sharing this because if you WANT people to think you're lazy or don't care what they think, then wear ragged jeans and a t-shirt. Trust me: if they think YOU don't care what they think, then THEY won't care what you do. It's very hard to earn their attention if they dismiss you as an amateur before you say a word. Why work that hard?!

Looking disheveled and sitting during a set,
looks and is lazy!

Chapter 3:

Is Microphone Technique Important?

That's a bit like asking a pro tennis player if her racket technique is important. The mic is *the most important tool* of a professional comedian, but you'd be surprised at how many beginners don't put any effort into learning how to use one correctly. They think they'll learn how to hold it, use a stand, deal with corded or cordless varieties, and how to avoid tripping over the stand or the cords *while they're trying out their first jokes!* That's a little like learning how to load your gun when the enemy is charging your position. Not smart, and possibly deadly.

The microphone gives you control and power over the room. There may be hecklers, but you have the only mic! Most managers/producers will actually *respect* you if you admit that you don't have much (or any) experience using a mic and would like to come in an hour before doors open to get the feel of it for 10 minutes ("Wow. This guy/gal wants to *Be Prepared!)* Remember, THEY want you to succeed as much as YOU do. They want the audience to experience as *professional* a show as possible so you'll tell your friends and they'll buy tickets and drinks, too.

A few basics: When an Emcee introduces you, nine times out of 10 they'll leave the mic in the stand for you. My advice is to start talking *before* you reach the mic, and continue some preliminaries when you reach it, e.g., "Thank you, thank you very much, great to be here." It offers continuity for the audience and is a lot easier for you. Keep in mind that in the first 20 seconds you're On Mic, the sound guy should be adjusting the volume to your voice, because everyone's voice is different!

Very important: DO NOT eat the mic—BIG amateur mistake. Yes, you see professional singers do it; but it is wrong for many reasons. It distorts the sound, makes you annoyingly loud, and you're spreading your saliva and microbes to every other person who uses the mic.

Proper microphone position is about three inches from your mouth. If the sound seems too soft, let the sound guy adjust it—that's his responsibility. Plus, while performing, you can always get an inch closer to "sell" or "push" a punchline. If you are "eating" the mic, you have nowhere to go.

Another example of good mic use is to hold the mic away as YOU get louder—i.e., "bim, bam, boom, BAM!"—which also exaggerates a bit without blowing out the system. Watch a virtuoso like Gaffigan on YouTube and you'll pick up some tips.

The Three-Inch Rule applies when the mic is on the stand as well, of course, but when is it appropriate to take it off the stand and go 'Hand-Held'? That's pretty much up to you—some comics prefer to keep it on and lean the stand as they move, but that requires lots of practice.

When and if you choose to take it off the stand, *carefully* slide the mic out of the clip that holds it in place. Don't break something being impatient or macho—that will cost the producer the money to replace it, and potentially cost you a future gig.

Once you have pulled the mic out, carefully (and *casually)* move the stand so it's not between you and the audience. It should be close enough so you can grab it quickly when a bit requires using both hands.

Some mics have an "off/on" switch right on the body (the part you hold), so be careful not to cut your own audio while performing. Most clubs "lock down" that switch, but still *Be Prepared!*

What golfers teach about holding a club could easily apply to holding a microphone: pretend you're holding a tube of toothpaste—firmly enough so it's secure, but not hard enough to push the paste out.

Longtime actor and stage performer Pat Morita *(Karate Kid)* always said to hold the mic "with your fingertips like a flute of champagne" so you look confident and professional. Pat thinks that holding the mic in a tight fist signals to the audience that you're angry or insecure—bad looks for a comic.

Important thing is to be comfortable and heard without blowing out the system. Trust your voice and whomever is running the sound board...you've got this!

All of the above can be summarized in two words: *Be Prepared!* which means spending some quality time with your most important tool before you hit the stage.

Hand held or on the mic stand, mouth 3 inches
from mic is best....always!

Chapter 4:

Do I Need To Interact With People?

As a producer, I was always amazed when comics or wannabe comics didn't bother to introduce themselves to me. I was producing the Open Mic or the show they wanted to appear in, using MY stage, and they didn't have the common courtesy to at least say hello!?

Look, I know you're nervous, but you have to respect the fact that you are in someone else's world. It's just good form and good *business* to introduce yourself and even thank the producer for giving you the opportunity to perform on his/her stage. If you don't make sure the producer knows who you are, ask about stage time allowed, when you'll be introduced, any rules about dirty or clean material, you can burn a possible future in the business by getting off on the WRONG foot.

Make sure you understand what's expected of you both onstage and off. Know where to sit or stand while waiting to go on, if complimentary drinks available (never drink before a set), and the Emcee's name. It's good policy to treat the Emcee like the club owner, because in many cases he/she runs the room and can dictate when or how your set goes. Make sure the Emcee knows your name and how to pronounce it. Pros often have a printed intro in a large font so it can be read easily in a dark club room (keep it *short)*, and easy instructions on how to pronounce their name if it's not obvious ("rhymes with Ankle," or "pronounced "GAFF-i-gun").

Ask the Emcee if there's anything you should know about the crowd—are there hecklers or trouble spots, any references to avoid? Sure, some may just blow you off; but just asking shows you care about the club, the stage, and the audience as much as yourself, and that gets you Big Points.

Since you're your own Marketing Department, have plenty of business cards handy (and a comedy résumé and 8x10 in a satchel nearby— you never know!). It's a good idea to say your name as you leave the stage to plant it in their memory, e.g. "I hope you had as much fun as I did, I'm Brandy Coleman, hope to see you again!"

**Remember, the audience is on your side.....
Relax and be friendly!**

Chapter 5:

Are Open Mic's Something I Should Do?

I have already stressed how important it is to be prepared for your early stage sets, most of which will probably be on Open Mic nights.

Why? Because every comic you've ever heard of got their start just like you will—by doing a number of random Open Mics just to get stage time and learn the craft. You have to understand that it's not as easy as just being funny, otherwise half the people you know would be standup comedians. You'll have to sell what you think is funny to a room full of strangers. That's 'waaay different than making your friends or relatives bust a gut! These people don't know you, have no history with you, paid good money to be there and expect something in return.

That is why I am pleading with you to be prepared and ready to present yourself as a professional. You're probably not one yet; but the audience came to be entertained, the producer has certain expectations of you, and you should have goals for success and lots of shared laughter!

Once you do one successful Open Mic, guess what? That just opens the door for you to get on every stage, take advantage of every situation, and perform as much as you can.

Most professional comics will tell you that the three most important steps toward becoming a pro are:

1. Stage Time
2. Stage Time, and
3. More stage Time

Sometimes you will rock the room, other times you might bomb; but every stage, every audience, every set is a learning experience that will help you hone your material, your timing, your interactions with the audience, and there's no substitute for it.

If you didn't know, some comics like Bob Saget or Ray Romano may seem like "overnight success" stories; but in truth, they both worked every stage they could for years before becoming that overnight success. That said, I can name 10 times the number of acts you have never heard of who rock comedy stages all over the world. They make a good living and do TV, concerts, etc. They're just are not among the 1% who were lucky enough to get what I call the "Golden Ticket," i.e., a TV sitcom, cable series, or a hit movie.

Famous or not-so-famous, they all started with Open Mics and being Emcees and opening acts. If it's good enough for them, it's certainly good enough for you.

Ok, your look is professional, you know how to use a microphone, you made a connection at the local comedy club or nightclub at an Open mic. What do you need now? Material!

Trying to think up jokes onstage won't work...
you NEED Material!

Chapter 6:

Where Do I Get My Material?

As I explained early on, I cannot teach you to write or be funny; I am a producer. But one Essential Habit I have learned from professionals like Steve Bruner and Mark Schiff: Write/Write/Write and then write a little more.

You should be writing a little bit every day, so make it part of your routine. Lots of your ideas won't make it to the stage, but a true professional NEVER stops writing! Look at it this way: if you wrote for just one hour a day, and that one hour lead to one minute of solid material a week, in one year you would have a 60-minute set (a standard slot for a headliner). Sure, it's a lot of work; but if you do the math and are diligent, it isn't too daunting.

One friend of mine, comic Ray Engan, even came up with a math-based "Humor Algorithm" whereby anyone can write to be funny on stage using standard rules of comedy. But of course, you have to WORK at it.

A couple more suggestions:

If you work clean, more stages are instantly available to you and you're ready for TV when the opportunity comes along. Believe me, there are more audiences for clean comedy than dirty no matter *what* your friends may think.

Be consistent in your writing and in your line of thinking. In other words, a comedy set is easier if there is a thread of thought through all the bits/jokes. If you throw a hairstyle joke into the middle of an airplane bit, you break the flow and confuse the audience.

Be yourself. Write about stuff you know or have experienced and chances are good that most of the audience can relate to them. With few exceptions, everyone has parents, has had at least a couple of relationships, has experienced awkwardness in social situations, and traveled, to name just a few universal experiences. Almost every comic has material on one or more of those topics, but don't worry—your stories and insights will be unique to you!

An unwritten rule of standup comedy is to open your set with your second strongest bit and close it with your strongest. That way you gain the confidence of the audience right up top and leave them with a reason to applaud at the end. Remember, it isn't a NEW bit every time you hit the stage. It is the same killer bit made to *sound* like it is new. That is how a comedy set is built: you write something funny, you perform it every time you're on stage, you hone and manipulate the words and timing until it gets a solid laugh every time. Then you keep and reuse it every time and then add new material that you should be writing and working on every day.

One last thought: never agree to do a set that's longer than you have material for or you risk a potential Death Set! Ouch! Always prepare (have I mentioned that?) and have more material than you will have time to do. Why? Because you may run fast, and if the audience isn't laughing, there's lots of deadly air to fill. On the positive side, the producer may offer you more stage time at the last minute, so it pays to Be Prepared.

Building a headliner comedy set is a lot like building a house. You start with nothing, build a foundation, add a framework, a solid roof to protect you when you're in a stormy situation, and then work on the aesthetics so it looks professional and is pleasant to look at. You keep adding and improving all those elements until you have enough material to fill five mins, 20 mins, 45 mins, and before you know it you have a headline-worthy hour. Jay Leno once did a concert for me where he did over 90 mins of material and probably stopped only to leave them wanting more.

The building process should never stop. A well-written comedy set is ever-growing and ever-evolving.

You are the artist, fill the world with your funny thoughts!

Chapter 7:

Can I Be Me, On Stage?

I've stressed how important it is to continually create material AND the great value of watching lots of other comics work (as Yogi famously said, "You can observe a lot just by watching"). However, be *very careful not to combine the two* and start "borrowing" bits, lines or premises from other comics. You MUST be original, or you'll be dropped from the comedy community quicker than Letterman could drop a watermelon.

As I've pointed out, we all have tons of *shared experiences,* from traveling to dating to parenting and school—trust me, *every topic* has been thoroughly explored. But you should be very excited because the world hasn't heard YOUR take on any of it! Your experiences and attitudes and phrasing are as different from, say, Bob Saget's or Carrot Top's is from Steven Wright's.

If you write, write, write, every day and pile up the stage time, your unique voice will eventually get loud and clear. Carry a notepad, tablet, or get a dictation app for your phone. If you're driving, or shopping, or even at your day job and something strikes you as funny, *record it immediately.* He who hesitates often loses a bit *forever.* Go back to it later and see if it's still funny or what can be done to make it funny. You might save it for months or even years before you get experienced enough to know exactly how to perform it. Save *everything,* and organize it so you can find what you're looking for.

Whether you write by sitting down in front of that terrifying blank sheet of paper, or noting things that happen in your life as they happen, or walking around the mall making sarcastic comments into your phone, there are opportunities to gather material practically every waking minute. And if you're true to yourself and create material strictly from YOUR point of view, it'll always original.

You'll soon realize that you can learn a ton and grow as a comic by watching other performers and never even think about stealing material. You can pick up tips on stage presence, physicality, phrasing, mic technique, and get ideas of your own. When you hear a comic's story about her nightmare junior prom, a light bulb might click on for you: "That date I had with the body builder! That could be hilarious!" Even if you didn't have a date with a body builder, btw. Don't let the truth prevent you from writing a great bit.

Be Yourself onstage; but still Professional!

Chapter 8:

Am I Up Against Other Comics?

By this point you should be preparing for—or already doing—some Open Mics or even stage shows. There will be other comics about to go on stage, too. They are NOT your competition! Trust me, as a comedy producer, I never compared comics or their material to each other. Everybody who takes the stage is there with a common goal: to entertain the audience. If your way makes the audience laugh, terrific, you win! But that doesn't mean the other comics lose. Just the opposite. As producers, we want ALL the comics to succeed, because then the *audience* wins; and that is the most important aspect of this business.

Actually, there is usually a strong and affectionate bond between comics, as everyone has endured the same crucible—there's never a shortage of Hell Gig stories when comedians get together! Sure, there are always a few who want to be left alone because they're arrogant or shy; but most want to talk comedy, discuss audiences or specific shows, and share comedy stories. In every way, these are learning opportunities. In fact, once you learn a few things (like from this book) you too should share the knowledge with others going through the same struggle. Remember, to a five-year-old, a ten-year-old is a genius.

Everyone climbs an experience ladder, some faster than others; but all have taken the same path. As was mentioned earlier, there was a time when Robin Williams did Open Mics!

So, in short, don't look at this as a competition. Work together and grow from each other's experience. Watch professionals, take notes, write, perform whenever you can, and eventually you'll grow into the professional comic you want to be.

Chapter 9:

How Important Is Stage Time Management?

From a producer's point of view, this is one of the more important aspects of being on stage. Whether you're a dancer, singer, actor, or comic, doing the time expected of you on stage sets the entire pace of a show. Running short can impact the overall length of the show, cheating the audience and forcing the Emcee to shuffle the lineup on the fly. Go long, and you may force other acts to cut their sets short, making them adjust what they've prepared at the last minute and throwing off the quality of the show overall.

As an Open Mic act, or even a comic in your first couple years of performing, you *have to* stick to the time you are asked to perform. If you don't, the producer will certainly notice and your future in the business could be badly affected.

Most clubs have a red light only the comic can see from the stage, or some other way to alert you that your time is almost up. At the Comedy Store in L.A. they shine a light on a framed picture in the back of the room. What the light means is that you have less than five minutes to wrap up. Always assume you didn't see the light when it first came on and start your closing bit as soon as possible. If you finish a couple of minutes early, no worries. If the light is on, you've done your job, and somebody else might get some extra time they'd like to have.

Many times, an act would think his personal decision to go long to satisfy his ego was more important than my plan for the show. At that point I didn't care how funny he was. If he threw off the entire flow of the show and forced the headliner to go short, I didn't mince words: "Do that again," I'd say, "and you are done at this club." And they knew I meant it. I made it clear that it was my club, not his #$!@#!%&! man cave.

In other words, "Respect the light, or get out of my sight."

From a Producers viewpoint, Stage Time management is the MOST Important!

Chapter 10:

Is the Audience There For Me?

NO! Every act should know and believe in their heart that everything we do is for the audience. I mention this because there have been times when arrogant acts have thought the audience was there for their personal abuse or to use as a Test Audience to try material. Wrong!

Every audience member paid a cover or secured a ticket (no matter the cost) and has every expectation of being entertained. No one ever promises a 100% successful show, with every act hitting it out of the park (I *wish*); but they deserve value for their money. Sure, you can drop in a quick bit or line to give a test run; but don't abuse the audience with ten minutes of untested material. It is our job to see they get what they paid for. It should be important to the talent, but as the producer it's especially Important to me. If I fail to provide the promised entertainment value for their dollar, they won't come back and might tell their friends not to bother. And even if those particular acts won't be back to bore the audience, the producer is there night after night, week after week.

So, for the club, and for the audience, you should ALWAYS give all you can in a performance. You won't always succeed, but you're entrusted to give it your best shot.

Remember, the audience is always right!

Respect your audience, always try your best; and that
positive energy will come back at you!

Special Photos From Back In The Day

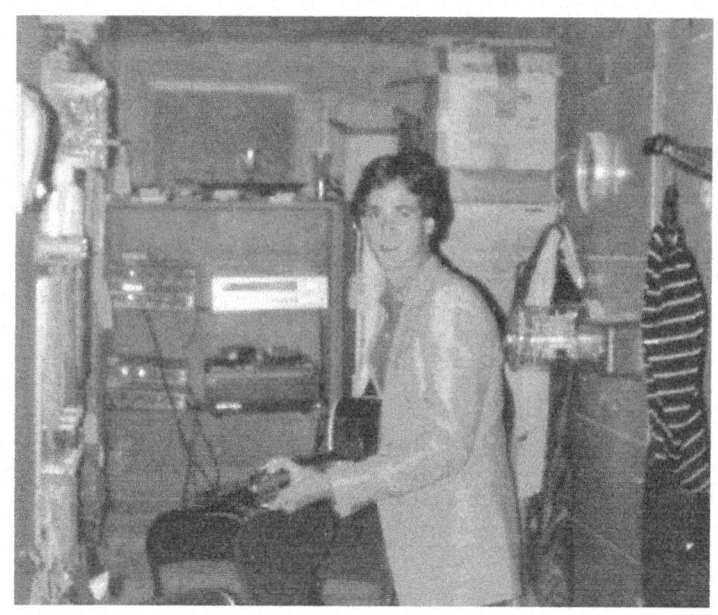

Bob Saget in our first Green Room (An electrical closet!)

Dana Carvey, my Son and I backstage at Ice House...

Jay Leno on the Tonight Show set with my Son & I

Bob Saget and Dave Coulier and I at my clubs' New Years Bash!

Emo Phillips at my club!

Tom Hanks & Bob Saget goof around on my stage as
Tom prepares for his role on Bossom Buddies!

Jerry Seinfeld, Yakov Smirnoff and I backstage at one of my concerts!

Garry Shandling and Paula Poundstone on my stage...circa 1984

Pat Paulsen and I goofing around backstage!

Bob Saget, My partner Bob Stobener and I working on
a TV commercial...circa 1981

Harry Anderson on stage!

Harry Anderson and Ventriloquist Jay Johnson
backstage at Laughs Unlimited!

Yakov Smirnoff and I backstage!

Garry Shandling as Opening act on my 1st stage...circa 1980!

PART 2

10 Answers You <u>Must</u> Know

Chapter II:

How Do I Look Now?

We discussed your appearance for early stage appearances and Open Mics. When you've found your footing and are booking little paying gigs here and there, you have to be aware that your appearance for every show is an important part of your branding. It is a consistent ad for the persona you want to present to the audience. I recommend that you follow the example of *all* the pros: pick a look you're comfortable with and stick with it. If you aspire to do TV, corporate gigs, and A-List Rooms, then spend some money and get your professional look together. That can be anything from a sharp business casual look to a uniquely eccentric look if it works and isn't off-putting.

Emo Phillips has a strange act, and thus presents himself in Floods, odd shoes, and usually a unique tight shirt. It all depends on how you want the audience to remember you: Professional? Business casual? Casual? Beachy? Slob? Meth addict? Loser? Creep? As mentioned above, once you pick a look (and it can change over time) try to stay consistent and grow your brand into a memorable image. I stress this because, as a producer, I know what will be presented to my audience *always matters*. I don't want a TV crew to drop in and see *Night of the Living Dead* onstage. I want to present a professional, clean look that matches the classy comedy entertainment I want to provide.

Again, watch a lot of acts on stage, TV, etc. and see how they use their look to sell themselves and their material. It is more important than you may think.

Looking Professional gets you paid as a Professional!

Chapter 12:

Should I Keep Watching Others?

Yes! As explained in the last chapter, it's important to study how other professionals present themselves. As you mature as a comic, you'll learn even more from watching seasoned pros because you'll start to see how they smoothly incorporate techniques that the average civilian doesn't even realize they're using. A few examples: proper use of segues to tie bits together; "call-backs" that refer to a bit that might have been performed 20 minutes earlier; and how they expertly raise the energy of the room until their climactic closing bit triggers thunderous applause.

Dozens of subtle details go into every solid comedy set, from the writing, timing, and pace of the presentation to the power of voice fluctuation and pregnant pauses, the nuances are practically endless.

To be considered a professional and treated as one, you have to realize this is a job with responsibilities, and the only way to get better is to work on every aspect of your image and what you share with an audience.

I know I've mentioned this already, but it can't be stressed enough: make sure you and the producer have a clear understanding of what's expected of you. You need to know where in the show you'll appear, how much time you're expected to do, if there's a group or special person in the audience you should mention, and if you're expected to schmooze with the audience after the show. Many producers appreciate the acts mingling with the audience after a show as it adds a personal touch the audience members really appreciate.

A good rule of thumb is to follow the lead of the other acts on the bill (the *sane* ones, of course!); they usually know what's expected and how to act. Hopefully they'll help lead the way as you grow as a professional.

You should watch other comics and learn...good & bad!

Chapter 13:

Do I Need To Keep Practicing?

Yes! Every professional entertainer knows that if you want to continue growing as a talent, you have to work and make sacrifices. Comedy is no exception, no matter how easy the pros make it look. They're relaxed because they've put in the work and have *earned* that confidence. You can't stop writing or you'll stagnate. Rehearsing your material to yourself or colleagues—aloud when possible—keeps you sharp and stage-ready. Don't think you're going to go onstage after two rehearsal-free weeks and hit every note perfectly because you know the material so well. Ain't gonna happen. You're sabotaging yourself if you don't practice. *Be Prepared.*

Becoming a professional standup comedian requires constant, incremental steps forward. One of the best ways to guarantee you're getting closer is to force yourself to perform at least one new joke or bit—no matter how small—every time you go onstage. If you're supremely confident that an untried three-minute piece will get roars of laughter during a 10-minute set, go for it. But you'll probably find that trying a single new line or a 30-second rewrite of a joke is a better way to make progress.

When you reach Headliner level, it's smart to have a marketing pitch prepared every time you go onstage. For example, if you're working a gig in Sacramento, there's no reason not to plug an upcoming show at the same location, or even one at another nearby venue if you get producer permission first. Building your brand means getting the audience out to see you again and again—another reason to keep writing and creating material. You don't want your fans to see the exact same show twice.

When I was booking shows, I always had my best acts repeat every three or four months so they could build a following. The result was larger audiences with less paid advertising and less work—a win for the club AND the comedian!

Stage Time, Stage Time, Stage Time...

Chapter 14:

Should I Work Clean?

The short answer is No; but as I mentioned earlier, working clean affords more opportunity and pay down the road. Plus, working dirty usually means creating harsher audiences and even more effort from you to control them. Yes, some acts have gotten rich and famous doing dirty comedy; but many more have gotten there staying clean. Ever heard Foxworthy, Ellen or Leno talk dirty? Well, there are dozens more who may not be household names but earn great livings working in the corporate market, TV, and more clubs than the dirty guys by staying clean.

It's just a fact that if you really have a talent for writing, working clean opens *many* more doors. Sure, writing dirty is easier, because a grownup shouting filth into a microphone is kind of silly to begin with. Similar to the kid who made armpit farts in class. People laughed, but was it witty? Clever? Intelligent? Corporate America doesn't pay anybody $10,000 a pop to make armpit farts, believe me. They want clean, smart comedy.

I always tried to book clean acts at my club because they were better for the audience *and* the club. I didn't insist on Prayer-Meeting *squeaky* clean. An occasional well-placed vulgarity can sell a bit if it's organic and packs an extra punch. But an act who can't say a line without four F-Bombs is just lazy, not very witty, and appealing to the lowest common denominator.

I can't say it clearly enough: working clean will allow you to work more venues, *classier* venues, earn you respect, and make you more money than working dirty.

Presenting a dirty, angry set; gets a dirty, angry audience!

Chapter 15:

Do I Still Have To Write Every Day?

Yes! One of the most important parts of being in show business, especially comedy, is working at your craft. At this point you should have established writing habits like setting aside an hour a day to write. Carry a notebook to jot down ideas and premises whenever one hits like a bolt out of the blue. I keep a pad and pen by my bedside in case a (rare) flash of brilliance hits me when I'm drifting off or waking up.

Writing every day is the best way to continually improve your current material and comedy set, but it's also the most effective way to make *continuous headway* on your primary objective of creating an hour of headliner material. As the adage goes, a journey of a thousand miles begins with one step. If you keep putting one step in front of the other on a daily basis, one joke and one bit at a time, you'll eventually reach that goal. Achieving it can take years, and the only way to ensure that you're getting there as fast as you possibly can is to *write every day*. That's why I stress it so much. Creating fresh, never-before-seen standup material is at the core of what you want to become. If you stop writing, stop being creative, what's the point?

Sure, doing standup comedy is a fun and creative pursuit, and hopefully you'll get a ton of enjoyment out of it. But it should be clear by now that if you want to be taken seriously as a comedian, you can't consider it fun and games. You have to put in the *work*. LOTS of work. Hopefully it will be work you enjoy doing for a long time!

Your first short-term goal is to write for an hour every day and to carry a notepad (or use a dictation app on your phone) so you can save any idea any place and anytime. Remember, this is all about and *all on* you. Sure, you can pay someone to write for you; but unless you are rich or too busy (very rare) all comedians write and perform their own material. So get to it, and let's start building a comedy career for you!

Carry a notepad or a recorder...you never know
when comedy genius will strike!

Chapter 16:

Is Connecting With The Audience Important?

Yes! In fact, it's probably the most important part of the craft of standup. Being able to grab the attention of a room full of strangers, connect with them in a funny way, and take them on a comedy journey is what you should be striving for. The really good comics have the confidence that—regardless of who is in the seats—every audience can be controlled, entertained, and totally satisfied with the comedy experience.

One of the ways that's achieved is by talking about things everyone can relate to. That is exactly why all the great comics talk about marriage, travel, work, cars, weather, dating, smoking, death, shopping, and a hundred other things we all deal with sometime in our lives. *Relate with the audience!*

After you learn how to manage the stage, managing the audience is your next objective; and that means creating material and jokes from everyday experiences to engage the audience and win them over. Comedy at its basic level is finding the humor in all the normal, often boring things we all deal with every day.

Seinfeld used to do a bit about how men's pajamas are always designed like a mini-suit: Breast pocket, collars, cuffs, etc. Why? "Will an important meeting break out in the middle of the night?"

Can you think of anything with seemingly *less potential to be engaging* than talking about men's sleepwear?! So why did it kill every time he performed it? One, it's relatable. Pajamas like that aren't popular anymore, but we've all seen them in ads or actually *worn by* our parents or grandparents. So everybody can picture them as soon as he mentions them. Seinfeld's genius is the ability to identify an arcane detail like that and then describe it in a way that *never would have occurred to the average person:* "It's designed like a mini-suit." Only Jerry.

In fact, it is often the simplest of ideas that can be made hilarious. Parking a car? Buying a shirt? Buying "pre-worn" stuff in a thrift shop? Trying to figure out what the waiter is talking about in a fancy restaurant? Trying to get a baby to sleep?

With inventive, original, fresh writing, the most familiar things can be turned into comedy gold.

Write, write, write, always find a premise everyone can relate to and you'll go far in this business. People who fail at standup comedy basically come in two categories: 1) Those who mistakenly think they have a talent for it, and 2) Those who mistakenly think their talent is enough. If they don't put in the work and creative time to succeed, their talent will come to nothing.

Not Relating to the Audience can Lead to Bad Situations!

Chapter 17:

Who Am I Working For?

"YOU" is the answer to this question. You are basically a self-employed independent contractor, and you are the product. As I've mentioned, this is a business, and you are responsible for marketing, product development, contracting, scheduling, and every other detail that has to be addressed if you want to be a professional comedian. Being funny is essential, of course, but your job doesn't stop there.

Unless you have resources most beginning comics don't, from the beginning it's your responsibility to manage every aspect of your career. Whether you are an Open Mic'er or a seasoned pro, several things should be Top Of Mind for you every single day. For example, while you *must* continue to work on your product—i.e., your material and stage skills—you have to manage your bookings, travel, expenses/budget, marketing your brand and gigs, etc.

There are loads of opportunities on social media to market yourself and keep yourself in the public eye if you learn how to use the platforms properly. You may even create a CD or book based on your comedy that you can sell or give away. Keep your eyes and ears open and you'll see there's an endless supply of creative ideas out there.

I stress this because many young comics do not understand how important the business side is. Quite frankly, if you don't manage the business side well, no matter how funny you are, you'll get stuck in long ruts, stagnate, and could ultimately fail. That understood, let's re-iterate what aspects of the business side of this career choice you need to be aware of and planning for.

21.　　**Finances.** This is a rough business with rollercoaster income and cash flow, so plan ahead: stash some cash and *always live within your means.*

22.　　**Bookings.** It is up to you to use the tools I mentioned, which include a professional 8x10 headshot (Digital), a neat Résumé/Bio, (most producers are fine with digital versions nowadays and would rather not fumble with paper) a website with a YouTube and/or Vimeo link to a Preview Video, which usually runs 5-6 minutes. You don't want to give away your whole act right away. If you have a complete 20 or 30-minute *clean* set you're proud of, a good idea is to upload it to one of the video-sharing sites so it can be seen only by people who have the link. That way if a producer asks for it, you can shoot the link to him/her so fast it'll make 'em blink.

23.　　**Marketing.** With your first bookings, collect info and promo that can go into your Press Kit. That way you're prepared with extra material for newspapers, TV, and radio stations you may be asked to appear on. You should definitely have business cards (*clean* is essential, *clever* is good, *wacky* can be unprofessional), and many like to have other swag like stickers, t-shirts, CD's of material as giveaways for the audience (if you're not familiar with the term, SWAG stands for Sh —t We All Get). This helps to build up fans who will follow you to future gigs.

24.　　**Be Consistent.** Bookers and producers tend to rebook acts who are consistent with all of the good business practices above. Audiences tend to follow comics for the same reason. If they don't hear about you for a while, they tend to forget about you and drift to other acts.

That's why you cannot do all the above for just a week or month. It should be part of your routine for your entire career.

25. **Be Assertive.** Doing all the above, some will say, is the club owner or producer's job—and they would be correct. But in addition to exceptional talent, the other factor that lifts a regular comic to superstardom is being assertive and doing all this yourself. You do NOT need permission to market yourself as a talent, or for a particular gig. On the contrary, all producers will respect and value your efforts to pack the house if you take charge and help with marketing.

I understand that most people who read this book will not go to the effort and do all work I am suggesting, and that's exactly why *most comics* aren't superstars. Those who do the work automatically jump ahead of the pack and achieve more success more quickly than the weaker, less proactive members of the herd.

Be the Professional that gets the Golden Ticket!

Chapter 18:

What's Next?

Glad you asked. If you possess a unique talent and do everything I've suggested in this book, you'll have every reason to believe you can be a successful standup comedian. Being a *motivated professional* as I've described puts you on a faster track than the dawdlers. You might go from Open Mic'er to opening act in months instead of the years it takes most rookies. You might leap from opening act to headliner in just a couple years vs. the five or more years it takes most acts. I've seen hundreds of comics come and go in my 40-plus years of producing, so I am uniquely qualified to make this guarantee: if you do the work described in this book, write diligently and relentlessly, put in the stage time, and sell/sell/sell yourself, you will jump ahead of the herd of wannabes and succeed.

If you're talented enough and work hard enough to become the professional clean talent we've seen succeed over and over, who knows? Maybe some TV or movie producer might see your work and say, **"Now that's a talent I can work with!"**

You never know—quite a few have earned the Golden Ticket and gone on to amazing fame and dizzying fortune. We cannot promise that; but we can assure you that if you treat it like a job, work hard, stay focused, and respect the stage and audience, you will certainly have a career in this medium for as long as you want.

Fame & Fortune can be yours, if you work hard and treat comedy like the career it can be!

Chapter 19:

What If I Bomb?

As I've explained, bombing is all part of the growth and experience of this artform. *Everyone* you can think of—Robin, Shandling, Seinfeld, Carvey, Saget, etc.—ALL bombed at one time or another, and probably several times. It's an essential part of the growth process. A reporter once asked Thomas Edison how he kept going after hundreds of failed attempts to make a famous invention work. He said, "Failures? Son, I don't have any *failures.* In fact, in only three years I have *discovered* more than nine thousand ways a light bulb *won't work.*"

If you're approaching your craft the right way, you'll find *dozens* of ways that your jokes and bits *don't work* until you hit on the magic line, phrase, word, or even facial expression. There's really no other way to get there. Don't beat yourself up if they don't laugh at a line you had high hopes for. That's not a *mistake,* any more than a pro baseball player striking out is a mistake. It's a learning experience, and the next time at bat he'll have a better idea how to hit that pitcher. In fact, a solid hitter in the pros has a .300 batting average, which means he gets a hit slightly less than three times for every 10 times at bat! And that's a GREAT batting average!

LeBron James was asked why he takes so many shots, and he said, "If you don't shoot the ball, you're never going to score."

Same thing in comedy. If you're not trying and missing, you're never going to score.

Keep in mind that sometimes *it's not your fault* if you bomb because a lot of factors can work against you: the air conditioner was clanking so the audience couldn't hear half of what you were saying; the comic before you was so filthy that he/she killed the energy in the room; a table of drunks was so disruptive that nobody could focus on the stage. Those are learning experiences, too, so try some survival techniques anytime you're given the, um, "opportunity."

I just want to stress the fact that you **will** have bad sets and good sets, and the goal is to practice, improve, and continually build on your comedy sets. If you bomb along the way, don't waste it—use it. You should record every set so you can analyze what happened and why in good sets and bad, learn from what you do, and do it better next time.

All the famous stars of comedy have bombed, so now it's your turn to join the club! Learn from your rough sets, accept them as harsh but invaluable teachers, and you'll go to your next set with a little more scar tissue & confidence, and a lot less anxiety.

Confidence is King, whatever shape it takes!

Chapter 20:

What Is Most Important?

Well, there's not a single answer to that. It could be Stage Time/Stage Time/ Stage Time.

It could be writing every day.

Maybe it's Respect the Stage and do the time expected of you, no more and no less.

Oh, and don't forget to be true to yourself, stay original and engage the audience—very important.

Could it be market and promote yourself at every possible opportunity? Very likely.

Or could the *most important thing* be to never forget what you want standup comedy to be for you, i.e., a *career,* so quit fooling around and work at it!

Okay, you're right, it's all of the above and more. You have to become a *great* comedian to be a *professional* standup comedian, and if you leave out any single task on the list above, you're making it harder on yourself, or even impossible.

This is a short book. Read it twice, maybe three times, or every couple of months after you've stacked up more stage time and have a better hands-on understanding of what I'm trying to tell you. If you're talented, original, dedicated to the craft and willing to put in the work, you can be one of the greats.

I believe you can make it. Now YOU have to do the same.

Now go get 'em …. "break a leg"

The Stage Is Yours!

Special BONUS Chapter!

How Do I Deal With Stage Fright?

By working with amateurs and professionals alike I've learned that everyone experiences some degree of stage fright along the way. I've been working stages for over 40 years, and I still get that terrifying brain cramp at certain large events.

So how best to manage your stage fright?

As you might have noticed, I highly recommend that you Be Prepared every time you step onstage--your primary tool for managing stage fright. Being thoroughly rehearsed and practiced—repetition is key—arms you with a confidence that allows you to kick that debilitating fear off the stage so you can have fun.

Try to perform your set in front of people—family, friends, anyone you can get to listen. Performing your material in front of humans helps in two ways: it allows you some honest feedback on your material (hopefully) and also give you the experience of speaking in front of a live person or people (the more the better!). Do this as many times as you can and as often as you can *before* gigs, and *between* gigs. Even your long-suffering, patient significant other can boost your comfort zone and confidence on how your personality and material will keep the stage fright away.

Another suggestion is mingling with the audience before the show, giving you that feeling of being part of the group; and you'll see that they are all just like you—a normal human! Ha!

I kid; but in reality, realizing the audience is just a group of people who could be your neighbors, co-workers, etc, takes some of the angst out.

Remember, the room is full of people who WANT you to succeed. They have a vested interest in seeing you do well, and want to enjoy your material. They're strangers when you're introduced, but once you hit the stage and start talking about things they can relate to and make them laugh, they quickly become a room full of friends who are ready to take a joy ride with you.

If you get onstage and assume everyone hates you, they will immediately sense that you're defensive and nervous and will react accordingly, taking away the opportunity for you to connect and share your material with them.

Many professionals will offer these helpful tips:

1. Be well rehearsed and prepared!

2. Before the set, avoid caffeine (plenty of adrenalin already driving you), use the restroom, loosen your face muscles & mouth, stretch, and basically prepare your body for movement on stage.

3. Have a sip of water before you go onstage and always have water on stage with you to avoid dry mouth!

4. As the Emcee is starting your introduction, take a deep breath, hold it for a few seconds, and roll your shoulders back—two simple actions that relax the body.

5. As you walk up after your introduction, acknowledge the Emcee by name—"Thanks, Donna!" which gives the audience that warm feeling that you're all pulling for each other, like family. That gives you a chance to show you're generous and can speak like a regular person before launching into your well-rehearsed material. Your brain gets the signal that you can communicate with the audience in that same casual, normal tone.

6. Next, with the confidence of knowing your material, approach and take the microphone or stand in hand and look into the audience for just a couple seconds. That helps you "feel" the room as you adjust to the lighting, audience, and stage landscape.

7. Finally, this is your time and your stage—you have the lights on you and the only microphone in the room. Take charge! "Hi, great to be here!" And here's a chance to demonstrate that you're talking TO THEM: "Thanks for coming out even when the traffic/weather/ electrical blackout/police chase/football game tried to keep you away!" Asking for a hand for the Emcee and preceding acts *can* be appropriate, but not if the previous five comics have already made them applaud—that's overkill ("Give yourselves a hand" is usually just a *painfully transparent* way to get a cheap round of applause, btw).

Whatever way you choose to do it, make an innocuous comment so that the audience and you both feel comfortable that for the next few minutes you're in charge, they're in good hands, and you know what you're doing. Confidence is King!

Special invite for serious comics....

I offer Private one-on-one consulting, so contact me anytime through my web site: **www.scottscomedystuff.com**

Keep'm Laughing!